MADDIE AND THE VIRUS

A Young Girl Navigates Life During A Pandemic

Author
Gretchen Susan Romanowski

Illustrator
Mike Rosado

Lulu Copyright © 2021 by Gretchen Susan Romanowski
All Rights Reserved
Published by Lulu Press, Morrisville, NC

This book is dedicated to my grandchildren who continue to amaze me, and to all the children and grown-ups of the world who have responsibly persevered during COVID-19 and demonstrated that taking care of ourselves and being respectful of our neighbors safeguards a healthier world.

-GSR

I dedicate this book to all of those around the world who've lost loved ones as a result of pandemics like Covid-19, as well as those on the front line doing so much to keep us safe. May Maddie's story be an inspiration for us to keep our spirits high even through difficult times. Special thanks to Kaitlin Peterson for helping design our little book.

-MAR

Gretchen Susan Romanowski is a semi-retired dance educator who has enjoyed a wonderful career as a performer, teacher, choreographer, and director She has been a dance teaching artist in public and private schools, universities, community programs, and arts academies. She has choreographed for the musical theatre and concert stage. Gretchen earned a Doctor of Education degree at Temple University and wrote her dissertation on Dancing Wheels, a contemporary dance company and school comprised of dancers with and without disabilities. Gretchen lives in Cary, NC and enjoys sharing her love of storytelling and dance with her great-and-grandchildren.

maddiesjourney.com

Mike Rosado is an illustrator, musician, and owner of MRC, a branding company in the heart of downtown Raleigh. His love of drawing started at an early age and throughout the years has been incorporated into much of his work. He's also the host of The Pencil Pushers Podcast, where he focuses on the love of the hand-drawn arts, inviting top-level artists from a myriad of different industries. Mike lives in Raleigh, NC with his partner Leah, step-daughter Mila, and pet-daughter pup, Winnie.

mrcraleigh.com

A Note To Our Readers

We have loved being a part of Maddie's journey as she's explored a variety of creative ways to navigate life at home with her parents during the COVID-19 pandemic. We've so enjoyed her spunk and tenacity and emotional strength as she's revealed herself to us. It's clear how invaluable Maddie's family and teacher and friends have been in enabling her to wake up each morning with a sense of security and adventure and purpose. As Maddie's journey has unfolded, we've realized that her story is one that is universal and timeless. This may not be the last pandemic or crisis we will endure worldwide. Perhaps Maddie's discoveries are ones that will provide a meaningful guide for all of us during difficult times. What is the message? It's one of reaching out to others – while digging deep into our own personal resources of resilience and wellness. We hope that Maddie's story resonates with you, our readers, and brings you inspiration. Wishing you well.

~Gretchen and Mike

My name is Maddie, short for Madeleine, a name which is much too fancy for me, if you really want to know. I'm 8 years old. I don't like this virus at all. Not one bit. I miss seeing my teacher in person and playing with my friends and going out for ice cream and having sleepovers. I get really lonely and scared and sad sometimes. Sometimes I feel like Pinocchio and Geppetto stuck inside the belly of the giant whale. I'm sure they felt alone and scared. It's amazing but by helping each other they were able to find a way out of the whale's body. I realize how lucky I am to have my parents and my teacher and my friends who help me so I don't feel so alone.

Mommy is a nurse. She takes care of patients who are very sick with the virus. She works many days in a row at the hospital and then comes home for a few days when she has time off. Mommy has a very important job keeping her patients safe. She says I have an important job, too. My job is to do my best in school. My job is also to be safe by following the virus rules, even though it's hard and confusing. When Mommy is gone, I miss hugging and kissing her so much. Luckily, Daddy is here with me. Daddy works from home now. His new office is in our washer-dryer room! He says he's a really good sport because he shares his office with our dirty laundry! Yeah, Daddy!

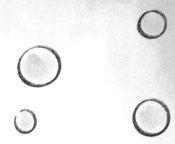

I'm trying to be a good sport, too! I want to do my part to keep myself safe and to help my family and everyone else during the pandemic virus. So, I wash my hands and wear my mask and I stay far away from other people. Luckily, I've discovered some cool ways to have fun and feel good even though I'm stuck at home! I want to share these ideas with you and maybe they'll help you have fun and feel good, too!

I really, really miss being in real school with other kids. Still, I'm doing my very best to learn in online school. You know why? So I can live my dream of building houses to help everyone in the world have a safe place to live!

Meet my online teacher, Miss Marie! She is so great. She teaches from her home. She has the biggest smile and gets us laughing all the time! She's very helpful and explains everything really well. My favorite time is when Miss Marie gives us a chance to just talk and talk with each other. We tell jokes and stories and do a lot of laughing, that's for sure!

Sometimes, though, I get really grumpy, like when our computer doesn't work or when my homework is really tricky or when I'm bored or mad because I can't be with my friends. Daddy helps me calm down. We breathe together.

We each take a big inhale in our nose (count 1, 2, 3) and then an exhale out our mouth (count 1, 2, 3).

We breathe three times in and out – slowly like a sleepy sloth – and then we give each other a big hug! Feels so good! Thanks, Daddy!

Each morning, Daddy makes me breakfast. My favorite is sunshine pancakes. Do you know what they are? They're pancakes sprinkled with blueberries and strawberries and covered with whipped cream. Daddy adds orange slices on the side of my plate. So yummy! Sometimes we even have breakfast for dinner. That's the best!

After breakfast, Gram and I do Brain Dance together on FaceTime. A long time ago, Gram was a dancer, and she still loves to dance. One of the dances she teaches me is Brain Dance. It's a fun way to move and stretch and get my brain and my body ready for a new day. We breathe, wake up our skin, curl in and out of our turtle shells, swish our fox tails, move our arms by themselves and then our legs by themselves, open and close like a door, stretch our eyes up-and-down and side-to-side, and finish with slow turns into a balance shape.

Thanks, Gram! Hope you have a happy day!

Gram and I invented another online fun dance that we call Build-A-Story. Gram starts by moving her body in all different ways while she tells the beginning of a story. When she freezes, I know it's my turn to create my own dance moves and add more ideas to our story. Then I freeze and it's Gram's turn again. We go back and forth until our story is finished and we're ready to start another one. We've made stories about flying bears, rocket ships shooting into outer space, magical dragons, sad monsters, clownfish and sea anemones being friends, trees that change into magicians, and much more. I love storytelling with Gram and using my imagination to have magical friends and adventures!

At least once a day, Daddy and I go outside for a walk. Daddy says it's important to get outside, to walk and exercise and breathe in the fresh air, every single day, especially now that we're all stuck inside at home. So, we set out on our walk. We walk a bit and then we do jumping jacks. We walk some more and do a bunch of skips. We keep walking and then do bunny hops. My favorite is when we walk and then do pirouettes (that means turning on one leg like a spinning top). Wow! Daddy needs lots of practice with pirouettes! We walk some more and stop to do jetés (that means leaping high in the air like a leaping deer). Again, Daddy needs lots of practice! At this point we're almost home and Daddy says, "Hey! How about we tip toe?" So that's exactly what we do! A goofy walk with Daddy makes me happy!

One day, when it was raining too hard to walk outside, I begin thinking about all the people in our neighborhood who are stuck at home like me because of the virus. I have an amazing idea! I'll create cards for our neighbors to help cheer them up! I'll call them "Safe Smile Cards." I'll put each card in a clear plastic bag with handles. I'll hang the card on the front doorknob of each person's house. Mommy reminds me that, because of the virus, I must be extra safe. That means I'll wash my hands before making the cards. Then, I'll wear gloves and a mask when carrying the cards. Mommy says, "When I'm home, I'll help you! Why don't we dress up like super-hero mail carriers and wear capes and crowns?" I think that's a fantastic idea! I'm so excited! My insides feel like a bubble machine filled with cheery, colorful, bouncing bubbles!

My best friend, Akira, lives next door to me and loves to dance. We've grown up together and tell each other our feelings and secrets, which is really helpful since we're all feeling so alone these days. We love to dance together online, after we finish our homework. Akira tells me about "Dancing Wheels," a wheelchair dance company that he loves. It's his dream to dance with them when he's older. Our favorite dance to do together is Echo Dance. We take turns. One person leads by moving however they want and then freezing in any shape they want. The other person copies. When it's Akira's turn, he does a bunch of spins and then freezes in a straight shape like airplane wings. Then I echo by spinning and freezing in an airplane shape. When it's my turn, I do a swinging dance and freeze in a bent robot shape. Akira copies my swinging and robot shape dance. We invent all sorts of Echo Dances until it's time for dinner. Dancing makes me so happy!

Mommy tells me something surprising and wonderful! She says that Akira and his Mom can visit us in person without masks because we're now all in the same "safe bubble." This means that our two families have made a promise to each other that we'll stay home as much as possible. It also means that we'll always wear masks and stand at least six feet away from other people when we're in the grocery store since those people are not in our "safe bubble." This way, we keep everyone safe. So, the next day, Akira joins me and Daddy on our walk in our neighborhood. Akira and I do more fantastic dancing!

Daddy, Akira and me were on one of our walks one day when we noticed our neighbor's yard filled with a bulldozer and piles of dirt and bushes around a small pond. There were lots of squawking geese, too! He said, "I bet you wonder what I'm doing, making such a mess! Well, my plan is to make something beautiful." What a terrific idea! Akira and I decide to make something beautiful, too. With his Mom's help, we plant flowers in pots on our front steps. Very beautiful and fun, don't you think?

I have another dance pal, my cousin Winnie. When she FaceTimes me on the computer, we wear all our favorite costumes for our different dances. Our favorite dance is when we're princess-warriors fighting off the virus. We leap and jump and swirl and kick until we fall on the ground, exhausted and laughing! We catch our breath and do it all over again! I love my dancing cousin!

Once a week, Daddy and I go grocery shopping. I'm always excited to wear my mask and be mask-twins with Daddy! I'm sad to see stores that are boarded up and closed and I think of how, one day, I will help to build new stores and new houses. I'm happy that people wave at us and are so friendly. I love seeing all their smiling eyes above each of their masks.

When Mommy has time off from work for a few days, we have lots of fun at home together. We read and paint and play games and do puzzles and bake cookies and dance. Sometimes, we make a surprise for Daddy. Once we made a long, long paper chain winding through the house for Daddy to follow. The surprise at the end was a big, gigantic card that said "I Love You!" I love that Mommy has lots of art project ideas for me to explore. Being busy and creative helps keep me happy!

I also have a new pen pal to help keep me busy. I've never had a pen pal before and I love it! My pen pal is my Uncle Joey. He's been in the hospital for a long, long time with the virus. Mommy says he's finally feeling much better. She says he loves the notes and pictures I send him. I can't wait until he's well enough to go home so that we can visit on Zoom again. Uncle Joey was once a circus clown and one of my favorite things is when he shows me how to make all sorts of silly shapes out of balloons! I practice on my own at home, but it's not the same as when Uncle Joey is there with me. I miss Uncle Joey and his wonderful balloon stories. He's really silly! Now, it's my turn to put on my silly hat and send Uncle Joey a silly pen pal card.

When Mommy's still working at the hospital, she FaceTimes me after dinner. I send her big hugs and kisses! We talk about the happy and the grumpy parts of our day. I love hearing her voice and seeing her beautiful eyes. She tells me about taking care of so many different patients in the hospital. I worry that she's safe but she promises me that all the nurses and doctors are very careful about washing their hands and wearing masks and special clothes. She shows me her covid nurse's uniform. She looks just like an astronaut in outer space! Mommy is my Hero.

Before bedtime, Daddy and I like doing yoga stretches together. Daddy is usually very goofy and we laugh a lot! His favorites are downward dog and whale. Mine are tree and pretzel and sometimes we make double-trouble pretzels! I love this time with silly Daddy!

At night, if Mommy's still working in the hospital, we FaceTime and write in my Gratitude Journal, all three of us together. Mommy and Daddy give me lots of good news. They tell me that scientists have been working very hard and have developed virus vaccines to help people all over the world get well and stay well. That also means that I can go back to in-person school! Hoorah! I can't wait! I'm so excited and I'm so very grateful to the scientists who developed the vaccines – even though I don't like shots -- not one bit. I'm also grateful for more good news - that Akira's Mom got her old job back as a Dental Hygienist. I know that Akira and his Mom are very happy and as excited as I am with all this great, good news! Then Mommy reads me a story and we blow each other lots of good-night kisses. Mommy and Daddy say, "Sweet dreams, darling! We love you!"

Before I know it...

...I'm fast asleep, dreaming of a world put back together – better than ever – with smiles and hugs for everyone! I dream of a world where people help each other and where we're all friends. Good night, world! Sweet dreams!

Glossary:

BRAIN DANCE:	Brain Dance is a wonderful full body and brain warm-up for children and adults. It is based on nine movement patterns of infants during the first year of life. It was developed by Anne Green Gilbert, dance author and educator, and can be performed at any age or ability level and in any location. (https://www.creativedance.org/brain-dance; <u>Brain Compatible Dance Education</u> by Anne Green Gilbert, 2006)
1. Breath:	Slowly and gently inhale through your nose and exhale through your mouth (making a wind sound); (repeat 3 times)
2. Tactile:	Wake-up the skin by brushing, patting, squeezing the skin all over your body
3. Core-Distal:	Like a turtle, curl into a tiny ball (hiding inside your turtle shell) and then reach out long and wide (reaching out of your shell, greeting the world)
4. Head-Tail:	Like a fox, make a triangle with your body, placing your hands and feet on the floor, and lift your hips high and wiggle your spine fox tail all around
5. Upper-Lower:	Upper = move your arms and torso while keeping your legs still; lower = move your legs while keeping your upper body still

6. Body-Side: Like opening a door, stand tall and open your right arm and leg together, gliding your right foot along the floor and reaching your right arm upward; gently close; (repeat on your left side)

7. Cross-Lateral: Take your right hand and reach across your midline to your left shoulder; repeat with your left hand; continue crossing your midline, reaching across to your ear, elbow, wrist, hip, knee, ankle, etc.

8. Eye-Tracking: Breathe and stand still; reach one arm straight out in front of you and lift your thumb; keep your entire body still while your eyes (only) follow your thumb as it moves side-side and up-down

9. Vestibular: Raise your arms gently upward; slowly walk-turn clockwise twice; slowly balance in any shape and breathe; (repeat turning counter-clockwise)

CORONAVIRUS: A new virus spreading around the world; it's called coronavirus because it's shaped like a bristly crown (from the Latin word "corona")

IMMUNITY: The body's natural ability to protect itself against disease

PANDEMIC: When a disease infects people in many countries around the world

VACCINE:	A special medication approved by scientists and doctors that helps our bodies develop immunity against a disease; vaccines are usually given with a shot though an injection into the leg or arm
VIRUS:	A tiny germ that can make people sick. ("Live Science Just for Kids" - https://www.livescience.com/coronavirus-infographic-for-kids.html)
WHEELCHAIR DANCE:	There are many wonderful dance companies with "sit-down dancers" in wheelchairs dancing together with "stand-up dancers." Dancing Wheels, based in Cleveland, OH and founded in 1980 by Mary Verdi-Fletcher, is one such company. "Dancing Wheels is a professional, physically integrated dance company and school for dancers with and without disabilities. Their mission is to reveal that the best expression of the human spirit through dance is by people of all abilities." (Dancing Wheels - https://dancingwheels.org)
YOGA:	Yoga is a breathing and exercise practice that began in India many years ago. It helps to calm your body and mind. It teaches different stretches and poses which also help build strength and flexibility. The poses are based on the many shapes of animals, such as snakes and whales, and nature, such as trees and flowers.

What Do You Think?

1. Maddie can't wait to play with her friends now that school will be open again. What excites you the most about returning to in-person school?

2. Maddie often feels alone and sad like Pinocchio in the whale's belly. Do you know that story? Do you ever feel alone and sad? Who helps you feel better? How do you help yourself feel better?

3. Maddie knows that not all children have parents or grandparents living at home with them. Who do you live with? What are some things you do together that make you feel good?

4. Maddie loves writing letters to and drawing pictures for her pen pal, Uncle Joey. Who would you like to be your pen pal?

5. Maddie and Gram enjoy doing Brain Dance together. It's fun and energizes their brains and bodies. Why don't you and a friend or family member try Brain Dance together? It's described in the Glossary at the back of the book. Have fun!

6. Maddie and Daddy love to be outside and dance while they walk. If you went on a silly outdoor walk, what silly moves would you do?

7. Maddie's Mommy is her hero. Who is your hero? What is it about that person that makes them so special?

8. Maddie's dream is to study hard and learn about construction so she can build houses for people all over the world. What are your dreams for your life?

9. Maddie makes cards for her neighbors and she and Akira make beautiful flowers for their neighborhood. What are some things you can do to make your neighbors happy and your neighborhood beautiful?

10. Why do you think Maddie and Akira are best friends? Do you have a best friend? What do you especially like about your best friend?

11. Even though Akira is in a wheelchair, he's like everyone else and loves to dance and play. If you know someone who is disabled, what could you two do together as friends?

12. Maddie falls asleep dreaming of a better world. How do you want the world to be better?

Made in the USA
Las Vegas, NV
21 May 2021

23434040R00038